Zone of Genius 365

(A Book of Life Lessons, God's Blessings & Inspirational Quotes)

DeneQuia Towns-Able

Table of Contents

Dedication

This book is dedicated to my three angel babies.

Neveah, John Jr., and King, remember to always be your authentic selves, love without limitations, and strive to become better each and every day. I pray that God blesses the three of you to be amazing individuals who make their mark in their own unique way. May your dreams be fulfilled and your heart's desires be given to you without hesitation.

Mommy loves you, always.

– DeneQuia Towns-Able

Acknowledgment

I give all glory to God for this work. He is the source of the wisdom, strength, and perseverance that it took to bring this book to completion. I am eternally grateful for the blessings and the path that led me here.

The biggest fear you'll ever have in life is making a decision.

Be careful who you share your failures and successes with; sometimes, people will misread your passion, and often, that could turn into hate.

Stop with the 'You gotta help me' mentality.

If you're an influencer, why post negativity? The energy you put out is what you get back. People are more receptive to positivity. Push positivity! Stop putting negative vibes in the air, expecting folks to take heed. If the message is toxic, it won't be received.

#bosslady365 #motivationalquotes #oceansflow #teamdenequia #femininepower

F*ck social media – my real life is better!

Our social media persona is often very different from who we are in real life, and the boundary between the two is getting blurrier. That unclear difference has an impact on our psychology – sometimes positively and often negatively.

Think about it:

- *Our personal appearance*
- *Social settings*
- *Body image*

These are the main driving factors folks battle within themselves.

So many of us want the blessing, but we can't handle the breaking!
Stand strong, firm, & most of all, have faith!

Seeking validation is a dead-end road to self-destruction!

Some folks be so dedicated to their crash-out that they'll risk it all just to prove to themselves that they're not the one who was responsible for the wreck they caused.

It's sad to see people like this because they're willing to leverage their own livelihood, family, and reputation just to make themselves feel good for the moment. But the damage they cause in the long run is what they are going to regret. Don't be surprised when God shows up and shows his hand.

Some people have main character syndrome. It's okay to learn patience and allow someone else to shine. It's not all about you. Other people have dreams and goals to achieve, too.

People will paint a picture for you. It's important to experience someone for yourself rather than listen to someone else tell you how they may or may not be. People's perceptions can influence your ability to build a bond with someone who may actually be more likely to become a good friend or partner in your life. So just be careful about listening to someone who's angry, filled with hate, or indifferent. Oftentimes, the real culprit is the person who is telling you only what they want you to hear. The truth is that there is someone, though they just can't be bothered with details, a smear campaign is more their speed, and it's sad.

Set a good intention for your day. No matter what you're going through, be positive and think positively. Rule your power. You are uniquely you, and you're divinely protected. Your presence is powerful, and your soul is felt by others. You are a very results-oriented person; just make sure you create and maintain a structure and plan so you can succeed and build a legacy for yourself and your family. It's important that you show up in your own world as the authoritative one. Holding yourself accountable and understanding who you are at the core will help you in so many ways. It's time to unlock the magic you possess within. You have the gift of dedicating yourself to your goals.

Manifestation!

Surrender to new experiences; the security you seek is there, and your purpose will be fulfilled.

Forgive and let God lead you.

You reap what you've sown in your professional life. The money is coming; great connections are forming, and your future will be filled with opportunities to make money.

Balance and structure are needed so you can reap the reward you deserve abundantly.

Provocative people be having a problem with not having an actual problem. If you are dealing with someone who has an issue with you for no clear reason, then it's not worth your energy or time to even try to guess or ask them why. Simply remove yourself from this person's life and move forward with your life. Good riddance to bad rubbish!

"Ugly people don't have anything to lose!"

– A queen said that.

I Championed That

Sometimes you gotta stop, look at your trophy case, and applaud yourself. It's important to take the time to step back and reflect on your accomplishments and achievements, and to appreciate your journey, because you've come a long way. Your problems become a lot smaller when you start focusing on your wins instead of your losses. Take the time to count your victories and your successes.

#funfact #friday #champion #rewardyourself

We all have fears that we pray we can keep far from others' sight, giving less attention to the lack thereof in hindsight. We all want to feel love. We live in a time where our hopes and dreams rely on comments, emojis, views, and likes. Social media brings death to the real connections we never thought we needed from the start!

An associate once told me:

"Don't let nobody dim your light!"

Thank you, Anthony Azaela.

I feel at peace.

True bliss is the only peace I want to ever feel.

My new man will never be intimidated by any other man. My new man will celebrate me, and I will celebrate him. He will love my children unconditionally and provide the security and genuine love I want and need.

Love and patience:

•   *1 Corinthians 13:7: Love [bears] all things, believes all things, hopes all things, endures all things.*

•   *Ephesians 4:2-3: Be completely humble and gentle; be patient, bearing with one another in love.*

•   *Colossians 3:12-14: Therefore, as God's chosen people, holy and dearly loved, clothe yourselves with compassion, kindness, humility, gentleness and patience... And over all these virtues put on love, which binds them all together in perfect unity.*

Forgiveness and kindness

- *Ephesians 4:32: Be kind to one another, tenderhearted, forgiving each other, just as in Christ God forgave you.*

- *Colossians 3:13: Bear with each other and forgive one another if any of you has a grievance against someone. Forgive as the Lord forgave you.*

- *1 Peter 4:8: Above all, love each other deeply, because love covers over a multitude of sins.*

Support and unity

• *Ecclesiastes 4:9: Two are better than one, because they have a good return for their labor.*

• *Ecclesiastes 4:10: For if they fall, one will lift up his companion. But woe to him who is alone when he falls and has none to lift him up.*

• *1 Thessalonians 5:11: Therefore, encourage one another and build one another up, just as you are doing.*

Some folks look too deeply into matters that don't concern them. Learn to mind your business, and resist giving your opinion until you hear the other person's side of the story. The details are always important.

I don't have to be everybody's cup of tea, as long as I fuck with me!

I've been a bad judge of character type person for the past couple of years of my life. After self-evaluation, I've found that it stems from the traumatic experiences I've dealt with in my life and my sense of wanting to believe that everyone I have come into contact with is just like me. When, in all actuality, no one can ever be me, and only a few people I come into contact with in this lifetime will have the same morals, values, and beliefs as I do.

I've come to terms with the fact that because I've been so nice, genuine, transparent, supportive, and honest with people who may not have had my best interest at heart, that's what made them want to use and play in my face more. So now, I approach my relationships with new and old folks I know differently. Everyone is guilty until proven innocent, and that's just the way I've chosen to see things from here on out.

It's unfortunate that, yes, people from my past and a few that still exist in my present will have to get used to experiencing a new me in some ways. My plan is to stay loving, authentically myself, and genuine. But I won't bend over backwards for anyone else, and that's what matters most to me in this moment. I won't do anything for anyone who won't do the same for me. I'm not available to anyone who's not available to me. And I refuse to chase anyone who won't chase me.

It's time to stop living for popularity currency and start building real life currency!

- BossMan365 x BossLady365

Own the moment.

The Price of Authenticity Is Being Disliked!

Don't let anyone make you feel bad about shifting your focus.

Taking care of your children and building a home are two different things.

Men, it's important that you lead and serve as the role model for your children that they seek from these social media figures and rappers.

Mothers, it's time to stand with, not against, the father of your children. If he can lead correctly, let him. If he is a good provider and can be trusted to lead, let him. Don't step on his toes. We have women out here who have had to be strong all their lives. So when they get into relationships, they forget to tap into their soft girl era. You'll know when you have the type of man who will never betray or lead his family astray. If you have a good man, let him lead.

Fathers, be good to your children. Be their protector, their encourager. It's not just about paying the bills and providing a home. Being a father means learning to be a nurturer. Kids have a way of changing you and making you more aware of yourself and how you interact with others. Be more than just a wallet; be a father.

Mothers, be more than just a nurturer; be willing to step back and let your man lead.

When you own something, you can own the hours you put in, but when you do not own anything, you're putting more hours in and getting paid less. The key is to create a way to make money without having to pay the middleman a cut.

Smart businesspeople barter, plan, and save.

Broke people borrow, scam, and steal.

You feel drained after helping certain people because they're draining your good energy. Sometimes, helping someone who has no belief in themselves deprives them of growth and accountability. Sometimes, the best way to support someone is to let them go at it alone and face the challenges they face. It's best to let them work it out and find their way on their own.

REMEMBER: You can't save anyone who's addicted to suffering. Stop bleeding for people who will live their lives as the poster child of a pity campaign.

Your drive and your life are inspiring to a lot of people. They see how resilient you are on your journey and how minor setbacks lead to big gains in your life. They've watched you so much that often times their expectations of you aren't realistic. They'll put money in your pockets you don't even have, a house in your name you don't even possess, and a car in your yard you don't even own. They'll watch you grind, and because you look like you're doing better than them, they'll assume you are. People want you to be successful.

I mean, can you blame them? From their point of view, you have to have it all together. I say that to say this: keep going, those barriers you're overcoming and those little milestones you're achieving account for something!

Friendships that feel more like family are a great feeling when you're surrounded by people who have your best interests at heart.

Opportunity will always come to you; you just have to be strong enough to stand in line for it.

I don't believe anyone who just shows up to sell me a dream. I believe in folks showing me exactly what they mean. It's about the action for me!

A Note from the Author

Some people stay stuck in their heads for the majority of their lives. Use this book of uplifting quotes, scenarios, and sayings as your guide in life. It's designed to help you escape the mental matrix.

Stream "Chances" by DENEQUIA on all platforms.

– Denequia Towns-Able

About the Author

Atlanta's DeneQuia Towns-Able is a dynamic R&B, gospel, and pop singer-songwriter, entrepreneur, and community advocate. She is the founder of Boss Lady 365 Conglomerate, LLC, her independent music label, and of JJ's Toys & More, LLC, a family-owned rental business that provides bounce houses and event entertainment. DeneQuia's musical journey spans R&B, gospel, country, hip hop, neo-

soul, and jazz, nurtured by her musical family, church choir, and classical opera training.

Despite losing both parents and later her brother Pierre Riley-Butler, her biggest motivator, music became her therapy and guiding light. Encouraged by Pierre, she released her album, *The Art of a Woman (2017),* and continues to create music exploring resilience and healing.

Her entrepreneurial ventures reflect her dedication to family and community. Inspired by her youngest son, King, who has autism, DeneQuia advocates for mental health and autism awareness. JJ's Toys

& More engages in charitable initiatives, including food drives, school supply giveaways, and support for local organizations.

Alongside her husband, John Able (Super Dad Comedy), she produces comedic skits and web series, including *Hustle Crime Unit* and *Setting The Tone with LMAO* (2023), while hosting *Live With DeneQuia* (2024)**,** a show focused on music and positivity. She has appeared in the Aretha Franklin biopics *Respect* and *Genius: Aretha*, and is producing and directing *LMAO* (2026) for Tubi and Amazon Prime Video.

DeneQuia has collaborated with artists like LL Cook J and James Worthy, earning recognition, including "Florida Artist of the Year" (2023), for her song *"The Mud."* A passionate advocate against gun violence and for community causes, she continues to perform, give back, and build a lasting family and artistic legacy.

www.ingramcontent.com/pod-product-compliance
Lightning Source LLC
Chambersburg PA
CBHW051248120626
46547CB00014B/1844